What Is the Threat of Invasive Species?

Eve Hartman and Wendy Meshbesher

www.raintreepublishers.co.uk
Visit our website to find out more information about Raintree books.

To order:
☎ Phone 0845 6044371
📄 Fax +44 (0) 1865 312263
📧 Email myorders@raintreepublishers.co.uk

Customers from outside the UK please telephone +44 1865 312262

Raintree is an imprint of Capstone Global Library Limited, a company incorporated in England and Wales having its registered office at 7 Pilgrim Street, London, EC4V 6LB – Registered company number: 6695582

Edited by Adam Miller, Andrew Farrow, and Adrian Vigliano
Designed by Philippa Jenkins
Original illustrations © Capstone Global Library Limited 2012
Illustrated by International Mapping
Picture research by Mica Brancic
Originated by Capstone Global Library Ltd
Printed and bound in China by CTPS

ISBN 978 1 406 23386 5 (hardback)
15 14 13 12 11
10 9 8 7 6 5 4 3 2 1

ISBN 978 1 406 23393 3 (paperback)
16 15 14 13 12
10 9 8 7 6 5 4 3 2 1

British Library Cataloguing in Publication Data
Hartman, Eve.
What is the threat of invasive species?. -- (Sci-hi)
578.6'2-dc22
A full catalogue record for this book is available from the British Library.

Acknowledgments
The author and publishers are grateful to the following for permission to reproduce copyright material: Alamy pp. 32 (© Jason Lindsey), 26 top (© Daniel Borzynski); AP Photo p. 29 inset (Press Association/Corpus Christi Caller-Times, Todd Yates); Corbis pp. 16 (© Tim Graham), 23 (© Photolibrary), 24 (© Jami Tarris), 33 (© Visuals Unlimited), 36 inset (© Joey Nigh), 36 main (© Paul A. Souders), 41 main (© George McCarthy); Getty Images pp. 20 (National Geographic/Jason Edwards), 22 (National Geographic/Jason Edwards), 31 (Dorling Kindersley/Nigel Hicks), 35 (AFP/Kambou Sia), 38 (Kevork Djansezian), 39 (Scott Olson), 43 (The Washington Post/Michael Williamson); Photolibrary p. 26 bottom (Age fotostock/David Cappaert); Science Photo Library pp. 19 (Chris Hellier), 27 (Pascal Goetgheluck), 29 (US Department Of Agriculture/Scott Bauer); Shutterstock pp. 4 (© Danny E Hooks), 6 (© Rich Carey), 8 (© Bruce MacQueen), 12 (© Rafael Ramirez Lee), 13 (© mdd), 14 (© Stephen Aaron Rees), 15 (© EcoPrint), 17 (© Bcubic), 30 (© Perry Correll), 34 (© Gemphotography), 41 inset (© Fong Kam Yee), Contents page bottom (© mdd), Contents page top (© Stephen Aaron Rees). All background design feature pictures courtesy of Shutterstock.

Main cover photograph of a giant cane toad reproduced with permission of Getty Images (2007 Frogwatch [North]); inset cover photograph of Asian carp reproduced with permission of Getty Images (MCT via/Wichita Eagle/Travis Heying).

The publisher would like to thank literary consultant Nancy Harris and content consultant Ann Fullick for their assistance in the preparation of this book.

Every effort has been made to contact copyright holders of material reproduced in this book. Any omissions will be rectified in subsequent printings if notice is given to the publisher.

Disclaimer

Contents

What does William Shakespeare have to do with over 200 million starlings in North America?

Find out on page 14!

Why do coconut palms grow on every tropical island?

Turn to page 13 to find out!

Some words are shown in bold, **like this**. These words are explained in the glossary. You will find important information and definitions underlined, <u>like this</u>.

INVASIVE SPECIES

Kudzu acts like an unwelcome blanket over trees and other plants. One of its nicknames is "The vine that ate the South".

In the southeast United States, a vine called kudzu has been growing very, very rapidly – and not much stops it. Kudzu is an example of an **invasive species**. A **species** is a type of **organism** (living thing). Invasive species are new to a region, and they grow quickly and cause damage to the environment. Today, a wide variety of invasive species are causing problems all over the world.

THE STORY OF KUDZU

Kudzu was taken to the United States in the late 1800s. Back then, people thought kudzu was useful, and certainly not dangerous. Kudzu was raised in nurseries and planted widely. Up until the 1950s, farmers raised kudzu as food for livestock. It also helped keep soil in place.

Yet kudzu started causing problems. The reason is that it grows very, very rapidly, including in places where it is unwanted. Kudzu can grow up the trunk and branches of a tree to completely surround it. After a few years, the tree will die due to lack of sunlight. Kudzu also takes up the space and **nutrients** that trees and other plants need to survive.

Today, the US government considers kudzu a weed and a nuisance. The vine is killing trees and crowding out native plants across more than 7 million acres (2.8 million hectares). Controlling kudzu is difficult. It resists **herbicides** (chemicals that kill plants). You can tear down a kudzu vine, but it only grows back – as fast as 7 feet (2 metres) a week.

USES FOR KUDZU

What can be done with kudzu? Getting rid of it completely might not be possible. But people of the Southeast have found all sorts of uses for kudzu. Examples include baskets made from kudzu vines and jellies from kudzu blossoms. Some people eat deep-fried kudzu leaves! One farmer harvests over 1,000 bales of kudzu for animal feed. (A bale is about the size and depth of a long bookshelf.)

WHAT MAKES A SPECIES INVASIVE?

Each **species** of life arose in a specific region of Earth. Although many species have spread to new places, only a few of them are described as invasive. Species may become invasive in places where they have no natural enemies or they outcompete native species.

Lionfish are popular fish for aquariums. But some lionfish were released off the Florida coast, where they became invasive.

CONDITIONS FOR INVADERS

Species of life-forms include plants, animals, **fungi**, and **microbes** (very tiny living things). Each can be invasive, and they can invade in different ways. Yet certain characteristics apply to many of the successful invaders.

No enemies

In their native region, species have enemies that limit their growth and number. In Japan, for example, kudzu vines are eaten by several insects that are not common in other areas. In the United States, kudzu grows quickly and spreads widely because its insect enemies are absent.

Beating the competition

All plants and animals have **adaptations**, which are special body parts or behaviours that help them survive. Successful animal invaders may have adaptations that make them better hunters or grazers than native animals.

In the Florida Everglades, for example, the invasive Burmese python is a fierce hunter. It has become a strong competitor of native **predators**, which are hunting animals, such as alligators and crocodiles.

Plants compete with one another for light, space to grow, and **nutrients** in the soil. Because kudzu grows so quickly, it is outcompeting native plants.

Being general

Some species thrive only under very specific conditions. A plant might grow only in a certain kind of soil. A bird might nest in only one kind of tree. An animal might eat only certain foods. But other species are **generalists**, which means they can thrive in a wide range of conditions. Most **invasive species** are generalists.

TROUBLE AWAY FROM HOME

It might be easy to think of invasive species as bad or evil. They certainly can – and do – cause great damage. But all species are natural parts of their own environments. Trouble only comes when the species are moved to new places.

For example, gray squirrels are native to forests in North America. There they cause no serious problems. But in the late 1800s, gray squirrels were brought to the United Kingdom. Their population in the United Kingdom is now over two million! They are outcompeting the native red squirrel, which now survives only in small regions of the country. They also harm native trees by feeding on their bark, especially in winter.

The gray squirrel of North America is larger and more aggressive than the red squirrel, its British relative.

THE DIRECTION OF INVASION

Typically, invasive species come from large, competitive environments, such as the tropical forests of Asia or Africa. They often invade smaller, more-isolated regions. Islands are very susceptible to invasive species, as are lakes and rivers.

Why does species invasion often occur in the same direction – from large ecosystems to small ones? The reason involves **natural selection**, the process by which species develop adaptations that help them survive.

Compared to island species, the species that arise on the mainland tend to face more competition. As a result, their adaptations often mean that they compete very strongly against other species, which is how they survive. When mainland and island species meet, it is often the mainland species that has the advantage.

Introduced vs. invasive

Not all nonnative species are invasive. An introduced species is a species that is taken from one region to another. Introduced species include the most common farm crops, garden plants, and livestock animals. Only a few introduced species become invasive.

INVASIVE SPECIES AROUND THE WORLD

Invasive species are a problem in nearly all regions of the world. The tables in this world map show some examples.

NORTH AMERICA

Invader	Description
Asian longhorned beetle	insect, feeds on many hardwood trees
Emerald ash borer	insect, feeds on ash trees
Eurasian milfoil	**aquatic** weed, invades ponds and lakes
Kudzu	a weed, invades forests
Nutria	rodent, invades marshes and swamps
Zebra mussel	aquatic **mollusc**, invades freshwater

SOUTH AMERICA

Invader	Description
Aedes aegypti mosquito	insect, transmits disease
American beaver	mammal, cuts down forest trees
Asian carp	fish, invading rivers and lakes
Farm animals, (goats, pigs, chickens)	mammals and birds, replacing native species on the Galapagos Islands
Wild boar	mammal, destroys crops and attacks farm animals

EUROPE

Invader	Description
Asian clam	aquatic mollusc, invades freshwater
Cape fig	plant, grows in dense mats on **coastal** regions and in forests
Chinese mitten crab	a crab, invades rivers
Citrus longhorned beetle	insect, feeds on citrus trees
Sika deer	mammal, injures trees and spreads disease

ASIA

Invader	Description
Giant African snail	land mollusc, can eat at least 500 types of plants
Lantana camara	land weed, can spread rapidly in many environments
North American raccoon	mammal and popular pet, eats most foods in many environments
Water hyacinth	aquatic plant, grows in dense mats on freshwater

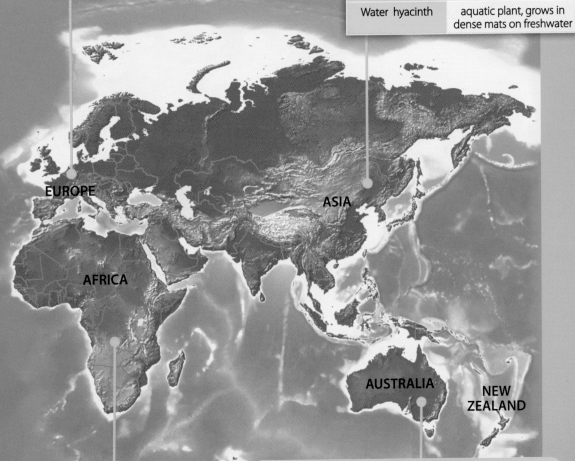

EUROPE

ASIA

AFRICA

AUSTRALIA

NEW ZEALAND

AFRICA

Invader	Description
Giant mimosa	a shrub, spreads across grasslands
Mediterranean mussel	aquatic mollusc, invades waterways
Paper mulberry	a tree grown for paper, invades forests
Water hyacinth	aquatic plant, grows in dense mats on freshwater

AUSTRALIA AND NEW ZEALAND

Invader	Description
Cane toad	amphibian, poisons native predators
Caulerpa taxifolia	a type of seaweed used in aquariums, invades sea beds
European finches	seed-eating birds, outcompete native species
European rabbit	mammal, destroy many native plants and outcompete native species
Fountain grass	popular garden plant, but can spread widely

HOW SPECIES INVADE

Today, international laws help prevent invaders from hitching a ride on aeroplanes and ships. But stopping invaders completely may not be possible.

Species have always been moving from one region to another. Species can invade new regions by natural processes and by human actions. Today, while invasions still occur naturally, human actions are spreading species at a rate much faster than ever before.

COCONUT PALMS

Have you ever wondered why so many tropical islands have palm trees growing on them? The reason is the invasive ability of their seeds, which are coconuts. Coconuts float in water. Ocean waves and currents can carry coconuts to distant shores, where the coconut sprouts into a palm tree. A new colony can begin to grow.

The actions of wind, water, and travelling animals are always helping plants grow in new places. Animals can spread to new homes by walking, flying, or swimming.

The coconut palm is a natural invader. Ocean currents carry its seeds to distant islands, where they wash ashore and sprout.

HUMAN ACTIONS

Humans have always been travellers. Over time they have established colonies, or new communities, in new places. These actions have helped plants and animals travel, too.

When Europeans began colonizing the Americas and Australia, they took along familiar crop plants and livestock. Some of the livestock included rabbits, cows, and sheep. Travellers also moved species in the opposite direction. The potato, for example, is native to South America. By the 1800s, it had become a popular food crop in Ireland and other European countries.

Humans have carried other species with them by accident or through carelessness. Norwegian rats, for example, were common stowaways in the holds of ships. The rats came ashore where the ships docked in North America, Australia, and many islands all over the world.

Today, humans are travelling farther, faster, and more frequently than ever before. Plant seeds, small animals, and **microbes** are often unintentional passengers on these journeys. This is one reason why species are now invading places across the world at a rapid rate.

HARD LESSONS

Scientists now understand how an introduced **species** can become invasive and cause damage. Several stories from history show how this can happen, regardless of people's intentions.

SHAKESPEARE'S BIRDS

A New Yorker named Eugene Schieffelin decided that all the birds mentioned in Shakespeare's plays should live in America. One of these birds is the starling. In 1890, Schieffelin released 60 starlings in New York's Central Park.

Today, the starling population of North America is over 200 million! They outcompete native birds such as the purple martin and the eastern bluebird.

Laws now regulate the transport of live animals and their release into the wild. But a lot of changes and damage have already occurred. Pigeons and sparrows were also brought intentionally to America, where they continue to thrive. So were many non-native plants such as English ivy.

THE MONGOOSE AND NENE

In 1883, sugar growers brought an animal called the mongoose to the Hawaiian Islands. They thought mongooses would control the rats that were eating the sugar crops.

Unfortunately, the growers' plan did not work. Mongooses are active during the day and rats are active at night. Instead of hunting rats, the mongooses hunted native animals like the nene, or Hawaiian goose. They ate mammals, reptiles, birds, insects, and the eggs of birds and reptiles. Instead of solving the rat problem, the mongoose caused problems of its own!

Today, mongooses continue hunting nenes and other Hawaiian animals. The nene is in danger of **extinction**, or disappearing completely, because of the mongoose, the loss of its **habitat** (natural home), and other factors.

DUTCH ELM DISEASE

Elm trees once gracefully lined city streets throughout North America and Europe. Some elms still grow there today, but most of them are long gone. They were killed by Dutch elm disease, which is caused by a **fungus** native to Asia.

The fungus reached Holland in the early 1900s. In the 1930s, the fungus reached North America in crates made of infected elm wood. Another infection arrived in Quebec, Canada, a few years later. Millions of trees were soon killed in eastern North America. Later, millions more were killed as the disease spread west.

Species of beetles act as **vectors** to spread the disease. A vector is a carrier of a disease-causing agent, such as a fungus or other **microbe**. The beetles that are vectors for Dutch elm disease are attracted to elm bark. They deposit the **spores** of the fungus as they feed on the tree.

Within a few years, Dutch elm disease can change a healthy elm tree to dead wood.

New elms?!

Elms are popular for their beauty and shade. To save elms, plant breeders have been trying to breed a strain that is resistant to Dutch elm disease. They have had some success. Unfortunately, many candidates are targets for other diseases that strike elms. The search for a new, healthy elm continues.

FERAL CATS

Cats can be wonderful pets. But in the wild, cats can cause many problems. The term "feral" means wild. Feral cats have proved especially invasive in Australia, where they hunt many native species. They also spread diseases.

Many animals that humans keep as pets can become invaders in the wild. Popular aquarium fish, such as the lionfish shown on page 6, are other examples. So are species of turtles, snakes, and other reptiles.

If you have an unwanted pet, never release it into the wild. Instead, see if there is another person or a shelter that will take it in.

Never release a cat into the wild. Feral cats will live by hunting mice, birds, snakes, and other small animals.

DAMAGE FROM INVASIVE SPECIES

How much damage can **invasive species** cause? Every year in the United States, invasive species cause an estimated $125 billion worth of damages. These **species** damage farm crops and livestock, fish and other marine life, and wilderness regions of all kinds.

DAMAGE TO FARMS

Johnsongrass looks much like other grass plants. In the 1800s, farmers planted it in fields because they thought it would be useful animal food. Unfortunately, it is poisonous to most livestock! It also spreads rapidly, and its seeds can germinate even after 20 years of being dormant in the soil.

Today, johnsongrass is one of the costliest weeds throughout the world. Every year, it costs farmers millions of dollars in lost or damaged crops. Johnsongrass can be controlled with strong **herbicides** (chemicals that kill plants). But herbicides cost money, too.

DAMAGE TO WETLANDS

The nutria, also called the coypu, is a rodent native to South America. In the 1930s, ranchers in Louisiana, USA began raising nutrias for their fur. Nutrias were also introduced to Europe and Asia. Unfortunately, nutrias that had either escaped or been released began thriving in rivers, marshes, and other wetlands.

Grasping claws and sharp front teeth help nutria eat the stems and roots of marsh plants, their favourite food.

Nutrias feed on wetland plants. They often destroy the whole plant to get at their favourite parts, which are stems and roots. Without these plants to help hold the water, marshes and swamps quickly return to open water.

To control the nutria population, the state of Louisiana has placed a **bounty** on them. A bounty is payment for a killed animal. Officials hope that trappers might kill over 400,000 nutrias over several years.

EURASION MILFOIL

Look at this dense mat of plant matter! This mat is made of Eurasian milfoil, a plant native to Europe and Asia. There, insects and fish keep milfoil under control. But it is invasive in North America. Eurasian milfoil is causing extensive damage, far beyond the damage caused by other waterweeds. Although milfoil can be controlled, it might never be eliminated from waters it reaches.

Milfoil is the feathery, light green plant matter in this photo. Its rapid growth chokes out native plants and harms animal life.

MILFOIL TROUBLE

Milfoil was once sold as a plant for aquariums. It arrived in North America many years ago, perhaps as early as the late 1800s. It has now spread to freshwater lakes, ponds, and rivers throughout the continent, from Canada to Florida.

In warm weather, milfoil grows into thick dense mats that can cover the water. They cover and shade many native water plants which die from lack of light. As these plants rot and decay they use up oxygen from the water. Fish need this oxygen to breathe, so fish populations drop when milfoil takes over.

Milfoil also affects many feeding relationships. Native fish, insects, and other animals are adapted to eat the native plants. But they don't eat milfoil, so the milfoil grows unchecked.

CONTROLLING MILFOIL

Scientists have been studying many methods of controlling milfoil. **Herbicides** are chemicals that kill plants. Herbicides can fight milfoil in a lake, but they may not remove it entirely. Some insects, including the water veneer moth and the milfoil weevil, will eat milfoil. They have proved useful in slowing the growth of milfoil.

Perhaps the most effective treatment for milfoil mats has been **harvesting**. Many states and communities in the USA have purchased floating versions of the harvesting machines that farmers use to gather crops. Others sponsor programmes where volunteers cut down milfoil by hand. It can be used as landfill.

Motorboats can spread milfoil from lake to lake. It is important that people who own boats look for weeds attached to the motor or the boat's bottom. Then remove them! These actions can stop milfoil from spreading even more.

DAMAGE TO NATIVE SPECIES

Plants and animals survive only when their basic needs, such as food, water, and space to live, can be met. Invasive species have these needs, too. When **invasive species** thrive, native **species** suffer. You've already learned about some invasive species, but now read about some others.

Cane toads cause few problems in South America, but are damaging invaders in Australia.

CANE TOADS

The cane toad may look harmless. It causes few problems in its native environment, the forests of Central America and South America. Yet the toad is a terrible pest in other places, especially Australia.

Cane toads catch and eat huge numbers of insects. That's why, in the 1930s, they were taken to Australia. Sugar growers hoped the toads would control the beetles that were ruining their crops. Unfortunately, the toads became invasive. They have no natural **predators**, they eat all sorts of food, and they reproduce quickly.

Many Australian animals are catching and eating cane toads. That's bad news because cane toads are poisonous, and often deadly. Because the cane toads are relatively new to Australia, most predators have not learned to stay away from them.

Spreading fast

Cane toads are spreading across northern Australia at a rate of 25 to 37 miles (40 to 60 kilometres) a year. They also are a serious pest on islands of the Caribbean, where they were introduced to help sugar growers there. The toads are poisoning and killing Jamaica's native top predator, the Jamaican boa, a kind of snake.

Eating poisonous cane toads is endangering the goanna, an Australian lizard.

GENETIC CHANGES

Every **species** has a unique set of **genes**. Genes control all the body **traits**, or characteristics, of an **organism**. They also affect instinctive behaviours, such as the way an animal finds a mate. **Invasive species** sometimes breed with native species, creating offspring that have a mixture of traits. In this way, native species are changing gradually over time to become more like the invaders.

The African wild dog is similar enough to domestic dogs to breed with them.

DOGS AND CATS

African wild dogs live in packs on the grassy plains of Africa. They catch and eat small birds and rodents, but also prey on antelopes and wildebeests. Except for their colourful coats, they look a lot like other large breeds of dogs, or like wolves.

The wild dogs are endangered for many reasons, including the destruction of their **habitat**. But they are also changing because they are interbreeding with domestic dogs, which are the dogs people keep as pets. Sometimes domestic dogs escape into the wild. The domestic dogs are also spreading diseases to the wild dogs.

Wildcats face a similar problem. The Scottish wildcat is one of the most endangered species in the world, with only about 400 animals alive in the wild. Now the wildcats are breeding with domestic cats. The species faces an uncertain future.

GENES AND TECHNOLOGY

In recent years, scientists have learned how to transfer a desirable gene from one species to another. From these efforts, farmers are now growing many genetically modified (GM) crops. With their new genes, GM crops resist pests or tolerate bad weather better than the original crops.

Although GM crops are not invasive species, their genes are spreading to native plants. A gene for pest resistance in lawn grass, for example, has appeared in some wild grasses. In Mexico, farmers who grow native corn plants are reporting the GM strain of corn in their fields.

INSECT INVADERS

Insects may be the most successful group of animals on Earth. Scientists have identified about 900,000 **species** of insects, and they think there are millions more species yet to be discovered. Insects can easily and quickly become invasive in new environments. Like other invaders, invading insects can change their new homes in drastic ways.

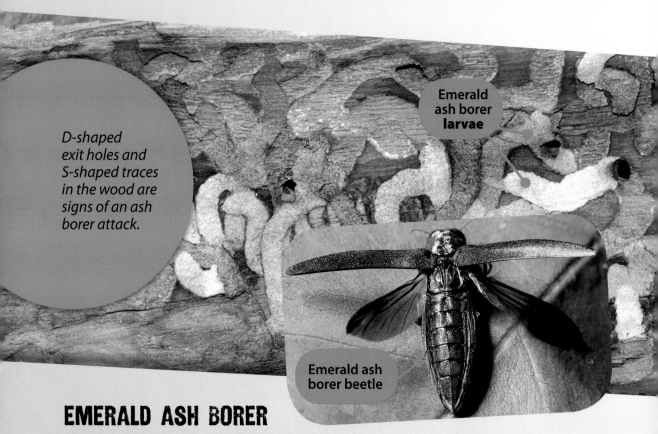

D-shaped exit holes and S-shaped traces in the wood are signs of an ash borer attack.

Emerald ash borer **larvae**

Emerald ash borer beetle

EMERALD ASH BORER

The emerald ash borer is native to eastern Asia. Before 2002, this insect had never been observed in North America. Then it was found in ash trees in Michigan, USA. Since then, it has spread to at least 14 US states and two Canadian provinces. It has killed at least 30 million ash trees, and the number keeps growing.

Ash borers burrow deep into the bark of ash trees. There they lay eggs. The larvae, or young borers, feed on vital parts of the wood. They kill the tree usually in two or three years.

North American ash trees fill many forests and are **harvested** for wood and paper. Now, over seven billion ashes are at risk.

Saving the ashes!

Scientists are looking for ways to control ash borers. Pesticides (chemicals that kill pests) seem to help. A wasp from Asia that eats ash borers may also prove useful.

Scientists also are collecting seeds from different types of ashes. They hope to develop a strain that is resistant to the borers.

LADYBIRD INVASION

Ladybirds eat aphids, small insects that eat the sap of plants. The Japanese ladybird is an especially effective hunter of aphids, and it was taken to Europe and North America for this reason.

Today, the Japanese ladybird is spreading rapidly and is considered more of a pest than a helper. One reason is that they eat more than just aphids. In the United Kingdom, scientists think that the invader could threaten over 1,000 native species. The ladybirds also tend to move indoors in cold weather. They stain walls, ruin curtains and clothes, and make a bad smell when squashed!

THREATENED BEES

Scientists have identified almost 20,000 species of bees! But in Europe and North America, the European honeybee is by far the most common. This is the species that beekeepers raise. The European honeybee pollinates the flowers of many farm and orchard crops, including apples, oranges, and other fruits. The bees also make honey.

Today, European honeybees are threatened for many reasons. Diseases are weakening many colonies of bees, and the bees are sometimes being replaced by invaders. Scientists are unsure of the cause. They are carrying out careful investigations to try to understand the problem.

AFRICAN HYBRIDS

In the 1950s, a scientist in Brazil was conducting experiments on different types of bees. Unfortunately, some African bees were accidentally released into the wild. These bees mated with local bees. Over time, their offspring have spread throughout South America and the southwestern United States.

The bee invaders are **hybrids**, which means they come from two different families. Some beekeepers in Central America prefer the African hybrid bees because they are hardier and better suited for warm climates. But the hybrids cause many problems.

The African bees are very aggressive. They tend to swarm more frequently than other bees, especially when they are stressed. They guard their hives fiercely, and they will chase enemies over long distances.

Fortunately for many beekeepers, the African bees live poorly through cold winters. Their movement northward through the United States is limited.

KILLER BEES?

The stings of African and European bees are equally venomous. A single sting is painful, but not especially dangerous. But because African bees often attack in large groups, they are more likely to cause harm. In the United States, their stings kill about one or two people every year.

The African hybrid bee (left) looks much like the European bee (right). But it is more aggressive and more difficult for beekeepers to raise.

WATER INVADERS

Lakes and rivers are valuable resources that provide drinking water, recreation, and beauty. They are also home to a wide variety of wildlife, including fish, birds, and amphibians. Yet watery environments are especially vulnerable to invaders. **Invasive species** can spread very quickly through bodies of water, as you learned when reading about Eurasian milfoil.

Although the water hyacinth may be more attractive than Eurasian milfoil, it can be just as harmful to ponds and lakes.

WATER HYACINTH

The water hyacinth is native to Brazil. It is a floating, flowering plant. Today, it grows in bodies of water in warm climates all over the world. It is one of the most harmful of all invasive species, partly because it grows and spreads very quickly. Its population can double in less than a week!

In ideal conditions, water hyacinths can grow to cover an entire body of water. They will crowd out native plant life and block the flow of water. Later, when the plants die, **bacteria** break apart their leaves and stems. This takes up a lot of oxygen from the water, killing fish and other animals that need that oxygen to survive.

SUCCESS IN LAKE VICTORIA

Lake Victoria, located in central Africa, is the world's second-largest freshwater lake. Its warm, **nutrient**-rich water made it ideal for the water hyacinth, which spread rapidly there. But in the early 2000s, the invader was beaten back.

How was it beaten? Scientists introduced two types of weevils, a kind of beetle that feeds on water hyacinths. Scientists are trying to reproduce this success elsewhere. So far, the weevils have not proved to cause problems of their own.

Today, water hyacinths have returned to Lake Victoria, but not in huge numbers. Weevils help control their population, as do chemicals and **harvesting**. Like other examples of invasive species, the water hyacinth is proving it can be controlled, but not completely removed.

Today, much of Lake Victoria is untroubled by water hyacinth.

Asian carp

Carp are a kind of fish that are easy to raise in ponds. They are an important source of food in many countries, especially China. In the United States, though, several species of Asian carp have been invading the Mississippi River and its **tributaries** (small rivers that feed a larger river).

These carp cause problems because they eat huge amounts of food. They can eat up to 40 percent of their body weight every day, and can grow 3 feet (1 metre) or longer. Native fish are outcompeted.

People are worried that the carp will arrive in the Great Lakes, where they could cause extensive damage. On page 39 you will read about efforts to keep the carp away.

Asian carp are now well established in rivers across the Midwestern United States.

CHINESE MITTEN CRAB

Mitten crabs reached Europe and North America in ocean-going ships. They have proved to be very invasive. One reason is that they can leave their homes in rivers and lakes, walk across dry land, and invade a new body of water. They also burrow into riverbanks. This can foul water-intake pipes or cause the banks to collapse.

In England, scientists are studying whether the mitten crabs in the River Thames are safe to eat. If the Thames crabs are safe, they can be caught and then shipped to China, where they are a popular food. Or perhaps the English will develop a taste for mitten crabs. People can help control an invader and enjoy a new food!

Zebra mussels

A mussel is a close relative of clams and oysters. The zebra mussel is a small, freshwater mussel named for its zebra-like stripes. It is native to lakes in Russia, but now has invaded lakes and rivers in North America and western Europe. Scientists think the mussels arrived in water that ships carried.

Zebra mussels grow rapidly on almost any surface, including docks, water-intake pipes, and even the shells of other animals! Because their larvae are very small, they can travel and invade some unlikely places, such as buildings which take in water from rivers, and water treatment plants.

If you look closely, you can see the plastic grating to which these zebra mussels are attached.

Humans have moved a huge number of plants and animals across the world. Most familiar farm crops and livestock are examples. So are most garden plants and many trees. Only a few introduced **species** become invasive. More than ever before, scientists evaluate the risks of introducing new species to environments. The right choice is often difficult to make.

A PLANT FOR FUEL

Every year, **fossil fuels** (such as oil and coal) become more expensive and rare. They also cause pollution. For an alternative to fossil fuels, scientists and businesses are studying **biofuels**. A biofuel is a fuel made from living things, usually plants or algae.

Which plants make the best biofuels? Useful qualities include fast growth, tolerance to extreme weather and soil conditions, and resistance to pests and disease. Yet these qualities also describe **invasive species**.

Biofuels now supplement fossil fuels. In the future they could become even more common.

However, the plant *Jatropha curcas* has these qualities and is a good candidate for biofuels. Its seeds are rich in vegetable oil, and the oil requires no special treatment to be burned. Jatropha can also grow in dry, dusty soil that might not support other crops.

INVASIVE OR NOT?

Jatropha curcas proved invasive in western Australia, where its use for biofuels is now banned. But in other places, including India and Southeast Asia, it is being raised with few reported problems. Many new Jatropha plantations may be started soon.

Despite the promise of this plant, scientists warn that it could prove invasive in many environments. They continue to research this issue.

Jatropha is raised in many locations, such as this farm in Africa. Scientists are concerned that it could become invasive.

OYSTERS IN CHESAPEAKE BAY

Oysters from Asia (inset) could help restock the oyster beds of the Chesapeake Bay.

Oysters used to grow all along the bottom of Chesapeake Bay, an arm of the Atlantic Ocean along the coast of the United States. The oysters were very useful. They filtered food from the water, which helped keep the bay's water clear. Oysters are also a popular seafood. In 1980, Chesapeake oysters provided half of the US oyster **harvest**.

Today, though, Chesapeake oysters are suffering. Diseases, overfishing, and pollution have reduced their numbers. Fishermen who harvest the oysters are suffering, too, as their livelihood is at risk due to the loss of the oysters.

AN INVASIVE SOLUTION?

Now, some organizations are urging that an oyster from Asia be introduced to Chesapeake Bay. The Asian oyster is hardier and more resistant to disease. People hope it will revive the oyster crop. But will it prove to be a pest, like zebra mussels in freshwater? And will it spread to other oyster beds in the Atlantic?

Scientists are struggling to answer these questions. They have proposed a variety of experiments to test this oyster in Chesapeake Bay. But once Asian oysters are brought to the bay, they may never leave.

ACTIVITY

LOCAL INVADERS

Invasive species are causing problems and raising questions in communities all over the world. Research an invasive species that is affecting your community or region. Find out the name of the species, the way it grows, and the changes it is causing. Research how people are fighting the invader. Prepare a report to share with your class.

FIGHTING INVADERS

As you have read, **invasive species** have been causing problems all over the world. The best way to fight invasive species is to prevent them from spreading to new places. Scientists, government agencies, and communities are trying a variety of methods to keep invaders away.

BIOSECURITY

Many governments carefully regulate the transport of living things across their borders. This is an example of **biosecurity**, which means safety from living things.

Regulations for biosecurity are especially strict on islands and in other sensitive regions. Inspectors search shipping containers and inside of trucks and cars. They even check the foods that an airline passenger may be carrying, and look for stray weeds and seeds on people's boots and shoes.

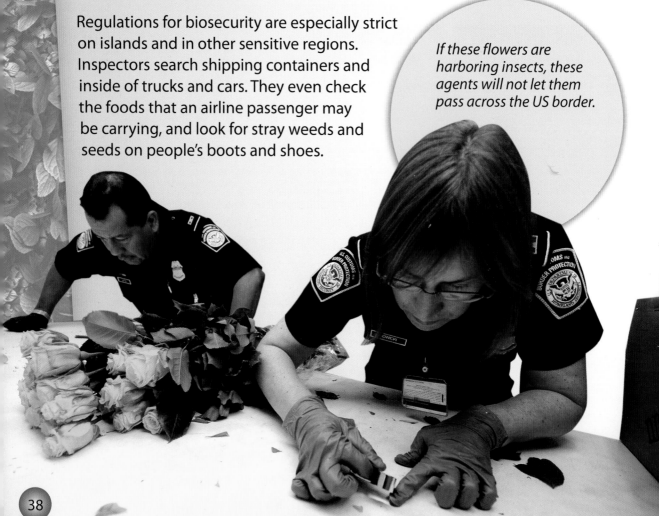

If these flowers are harboring insects, these agents will not let them pass across the US border.

EDUCATION

In the past, people spread invasive species through carelessness and ignorance. Today, education is helping people act more wisely.

At docks on freshwater lakes, signs tell boaters to remove weeds and drain wastewater from their boats. This helps slow the spread of water invaders. Many pet stores and veterinarians advise pet owners to keep their pets indoors.

BARRIERS

Asian carp are now thriving in the Mississippi River and its **tributaries**. But they have not reached the Great Lakes yet, which is good news. Scientists fear the invaders would destroy the Great Lakes fishing industry, which is valued at $7 billion.

To contain the Asian carp, the US government erected an electric fish barrier in a shipping canal through Chicago, Illinois. This canal serves as the water connection between the Mississippi River and the Great Lakes. In 2009, when the barrier needed maintenance, poison was dumped in the canal to kill the fish there.

The Chicago Shipping and Sanitary Canal could be the gateway for Asian carp to invade the Great Lakes.

39

AFTER THE INVADERS ARRIVE

How can invasive species be fought after they have arrived in an area? Each invasive species is unique, and different methods have proved effective in different cases. However, no method is perfect. Each method has benefits and drawbacks, and none has removed invaders permanently. Read below to see some ways to combat invasive species.

Introduce a predator

In their native **habitats**, many invasive species have a **predator** that keeps their populations in check. In theory, these enemies could work elsewhere, too. But the enemy could prove invasive, as well.

For example, garlic mustard is an invasive weed in forests across the United States. To fight it, scientists are studying a **species** of weevil that is the weed's natural enemy in Europe. Weevils are a type of small beetle. The concern is that the weevil itself could become invasive.

Spray with chemicals

Every growing season, many farmers spend large sums of money on **pesticides** and **herbicides**. These chemicals can work equally well on invaders and native species. But their effects are only temporary. Another problem is that, over time, the pests and unwanted plants and weeds can develop resistance to the chemicals.

Kill by hand

Do you grow flowers or vegetables in a garden? If so, you may have experience pulling up weeds by hand so that wanted plants can grow better. Many people are controlling invaders in a similar way.

In Massachusetts, on the Charles River, volunteers working in canoes pull out mats of water chestnut, an invasive weed in the river. In Australia, communities pay **bounties** on cane toads, feral cats, feral pigs, and other invaders. In England, some citizens are catching grey squirrels, the invader that is harming the native red squirrel.

Lack of insect enemies, such as the weevil pictured below, is one reason why garlic mustard has successfully invaded forests across the United States.

SUMMARY

Species have always spread from one region to another, usually without causing problems. But an **invasive species** spreads rapidly in its new home, damaging native species and the environment.

Humans spread species deliberately and through carelessness. Human actions have spread invasive species to environments all over the world.

Examples of invasive species include plants, such as Eurasian milfoil and garlic mustard; animals, such as cane toads and nutrias; and **fungi**, such as the cause of Dutch elm disease.

Invasive species can spread rapidly when their new environments lack their natural enemies. Introducing these enemies into the environments sometimes helps control the invaders.

When invasive species thrive, native species suffer. The invaders often use the food, water, light, or space that native species need to survive.

Once an invasive species arrives, it can prove difficult to control and impossible to remove completely.

WHAT CAN YOU DO TO HELP?

- Keep pets indoors. Never release an unwanted pet or aquarium animal into the wild.

- If you go boating, make sure the boat is free of weeds before and after you put it in the water.

- If you travel, follow laws against transporting animals, plants, and food. Invasive insects can hitch a ride on a piece of fruit! If you walked in the mud, wash your shoes before heading home.

- Learn to recognize the invasive plants and animals that affect your region. Many invasive weeds are easy to identify and remove.

- Learn more about **invasive species** and the ways that scientists are fighting them. New issues, discoveries, and ideas are in the news every day.

Tearing down invasive vines is sometimes the only way to fight them.

Glossary

adaptation body structure or behaviour that helps a plant or animal survive in its environment

aquatic relating to water

bacteria single-celled microorganism

biofuel fuel that is obtained from living things, such as plants or algae

biosecurity preventing invasive species or other harmful organisms from entering new places

bounty price paid for the capture of an unwanted organism, typically an animal

coastal relating to or near a coast

extinction death of all members of a species

fossil fuel type of fuel, such as coal, oil, or natural gas, that forms from the remains of ancient plants and animals

fungus (pl. fungi) group of plant-like organisms that produce spores, such as mushrooms

gene unit that controls inborn traits, and that is passed from parents to offspring

generalist species that can thrive under a wide range of conditions or eat a wide variety of foods

genetically modified (GM) living thing that has its genes artificially changed or altered, often by the addition of a gene from another species

habitat environment in which an organism lives

harvest gathering something, such as a crop. Harvesting is usually done to collect a type of food or other useful product.

herbicide chemical that kills plants

hybrid organism produced from two different types or strains of its species

invasive species species that grows or spreads with few limits in a new environment, causing changes and damage to that environment

larva (pl. larvae) young form of many insects

microbe very tiny living thing

mollusc group of animals, most of which have shells

natural selection process by which species develop adaptations that help them survive

nutrient substance a living thing needs to survive

organism individual living thing

pesticide chemical that kills pests

predator animal that hunts and eats other animals

species type of living thing, or organism

spore tiny reproductive unit released by fungi

trait characteristic or property of a living thing, such as height, colour, or shape

tributaries small rivers that feed a larger river

vector organism that transmits a disease

Find out more

Books

Alien Invasion: Invasive Species Become Major Menaces (Current Science) by Cari Jackson (Gareth Stevens Publishing, 2009)

Asian Carp (Animal Invaders) by Barbara Somervill (Cherry Lake Publishing, 2008)

Cane Toads and Other Rogue Species by Karl Weber (PublicAffairs, 2010)

Honey Bees: Letters from the Hive by Stephen Buchmann (Delacorte Press, 2010)

Invasive Terrestrial Plants (Invasive Species) by Suellen May (Chelsea House Publishers, 2006)

Science Warriors: The Battle Against Invasive Species (Scientists in the Field) by Sneed B. Collars (Houghton Mifflin Harcourt, 2008)

Websites

http://animaldiversity.ummz.umich.edu/site/index.html
This website has a huge online encyclopedia of animals, searchable by the name of species or class.

www.invasive.org
Check out this website to read the latest news about invasive species around the world.

www.protectyourwaters.net
Learn how you can stop aquatic hitchhikers! Use the toolbar on this website to find special sections of the site for your region.

www.feralcat.com
Never release a pet into the wild! Read about feral cats and the problems they can cause on this website.

www.worldwildlife.org
Check out this website to read about the issues affecting wildlife all over the world, and ways that you can help wildlife.

Topics to Research

Invasive plants in your neighbourhood?

Do you know which plants are growing in your neighbourhood, or even in your backyard? Take a pen and sketchbook with you, or a digital camera, and inventory at least five wild plants that you find in your neighbourhood. Invaders are not likely to be trees or garden plants, but they could be weeds.

Feral cats

Are feral cats a problem in your community? Find out by interviewing officials at an animal shelter or the animal control officer of the police department. Share your findings with classmates.

Healthy waters

What ponds, lakes, rivers, or other bodies of water are important parts of your community? How have they changed during the past 5, 10, or 25 years? Are they now home to invasive plants or animals? Prepare a report and share your findings with the class.

Fighting invaders

Research how people are fighting an invasive species that affects your community. Do you have ideas to help the fight? Make a poster to share your ideas and educate the public.

Index